# LISBON

1992

Edições MARGRAP
Av. Coronel Eduardo Galhardo, 6, 2.º-Dt.º
1100 LISBOA


Portuguese, English, French, Italian, German
and Spanish versions

English translation
**Walter de Carvalho**
*MA in English and German Philologies*

AUTOR: Adérito Tavares ● EDITOR: Mário Afonso Isidoro — Edições MAR-
GRAP ● IMPRESSÃO: Costa & Valério, Impressores ● DIREITOS RESERVA-
DOS: Mário Afonso Isidoro, Av. Coronel Eduardo Galhardo, 6, 2.º-Dt.º, 1100
LISBOA ● DEPÓSITO LEGAL N.º 16158/87

MARGRAP EDITIONS

# LISBON

## HISTORICAL AND TOURIST GUIDE

**Adérito Tavares**
*MA in History*

*Lisbon in the 16th century. Illumination from the Chronicle of King Afonso Henriques by Duarte Galvão (Museum Castro Guimarães, Cascais).*

*Terreiro do Paço (now Pra do Comércio) in the 17 century. Picture from the M seum of the City (painting).*

*The Casa dos Bicos before t earthquake of 1755. A 16 century wall tile panel (Museu of the City). On the right, fish market.*

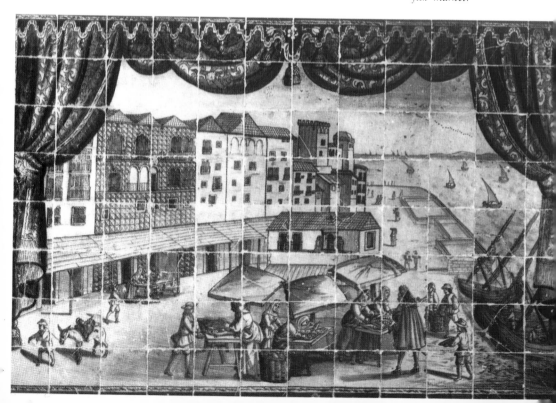

# LISBON

## The city and its history

    The origins of the city of Lisbon are uncertain. A legend ascribes the foundation of the primitive *Olisipo* to the Greek Ulisses, but there is not any reason for this hypothesis. The only connection is in the resemblance of the name. More probably, Lisbon would have been in the beginning a Phoenician colony (*Alis Ubbo*, which means mild creek). We know for certain that Lisbon was an important Roman municipality: *Felicitas Julia Olisipo*. The Roman conquerors/arrived at the Peninsula in the 3rd century B.C. The Roman city only occupied the hill where St. George's Castle is situated and its south slope.

    The Romans fortified Lisbon in the year 137 B.C. and changed it into one of the most important urban centres of the Peninsula. There are some remains of the Roman period in the city: a theatre, the public baths, numerous engraved stones and other archaeological material.

    The Visigoths, a people of German origin, occupied the Peninsula in the 5th century. Lisbon did not keep many signs of the Goths, which went on to the 8th century. In 711, the Arabs, coming from Northern Africa, settled here. The Arabian presence in the Peninsula contributed to a remarkable economic and cultural development. Unfortunately, the remains of the Arabian period in the city of Lisbon are scarce. The Mohammedan, besides improving the fortifications in the area of the Alcáçova of the Castle (later called St. George), surrounded the city with an excellent wall, the *Old Wall*, or *Moorish Wall*, of which there are still some remains. Next to the Moorish Wall, on the east side, still at the time of the Mohammedan dominion, a district whose name means hot springs or public baths in Arab would develop: *Al Hamma* (Alfama). In fact, there were public baths in Alfama, until a few years ago.

After the Mohammedan conquest, the Christian of the Peninsula, who took shelter in the North, started the reconquest. By the middle of the 12th century Portugal was already settled. In 1147, Afonso Henriques, the first King of Portugal, conquested Lisbon to the Moors. The city eliminated all the remains of the Mohammedan occupation when it became Portuguese and Christian. The mosques were replaced by churches. The cathedral of Lisbon was built in the 12th century.

The surviving Moors were forced to live in a particular district, the *Mouraria*, situated in the Northern part of the hill of the Castle.

By the end of the 14th century, the city had enlarged beyond the old Mohammedan wall. Besides the districts of Alfama and Mouraria, the urban tissue started settling in the area of the City centre (*Baixa*). The *Baixa* occupied the place of an old tributary of the river Tagus, marshy and wet, that, meanwhile, was silted up.

At the beginning of the 13th century, Lisbon had a population of 15 000 inhabitants. Although it was one of the most important cities in the country, together with Oporto, Braga, Coimbra and Evora, it was not the capital city. The first Portuguese monarchs had an itinerant court. They settled themselves periodically where the needs of the Reconquest or administration demanded it. In fact, only at the end of the 14th century, in the reign of King Fernando, did Lisbon become the definitive capital of the country. It was also King Fernando who, in 1373, built a new wall around Lisbon, to protect the districts that in the meantime had been built.

The Casa dos Bicos *after the*
*restoration in 1983.*

*Aerial view of the area of St.*
*George's Castle. On the right,*
*Alfama. In the distance, St.*
*Vincent church.*

Two details of St. George's Castle: Northern Gate; battlements of the Tower Cistern and, in the distance, St. Vincent's church.

View of the City from the Castle.

Inside of St. George's Castle (Castelejo).

Alfama in the beginning of the 20th century. A watercolour by Roque Gameiro, existent in the Museum of the City.

A characteristic house, at Largo do Menino de Deus. It is one of the 16th century rare houses still existent in Lisbon.

This wall was to be precious in the defense against the Castilian siege that the city suffered, during the Revolution of 1383-85.

After this disturbing period in the history of Portugal, the maritime expansion of the 15th and 16th centuries opened new routes to the city. Lisbon becomes then an important business mart, especially after the discorvering of the maritime route to India, in 1498. The prosperity provided by the trade of the Eastern spices, although short, allowed Lisbon to be enriched with some of its most beautiful monuments. King Manuel I (1495-1521) built a magnificent palace near the river, to replace his old royal residence, situated in the Castle (the Palace of the Alcáçova of St. George's

*Alfama: characteristic street.*

F. Gerardo

*The* varinas *were fishwives who went along the streets of Lisbon selling fish. They were more popular in the oldest quarters. Nowadays they have almost disappeared. (Water-colour by F. Gerardo).*

Castle). It was the new palace — the Palace (*Paço*) of the River — which gave the name to the *Terreiro do Paço, Praça do Comércio* nowadays. It was also in this period that the Monastery of Jerónimos and the Tower of Belém were built.

The city, attracted to the river by the maritime trade from overseas, grew now towards the West. At the end of the 16th century, Lisbon already had a population of about 100 thousand inhabitans, being an important centre of attraction for the people living in the countryside. In the 17th century, the growth is emphasized. Little by little, Lisbon became a city of hills, occupying the hills of the neighbourhood (in all there are about twenty, nowadays).

New religious and civilian buildings in the baroque style appeared. The first district of straight streets, geometrically drawn, is born — the *Bairro Alto*, one of the most picturesque of the city nowadays.

When the Eastern trade declined, the Portuguese turned to Brazil. Sugar and tabacco replaced spices in the 17th century. It is thanks to the profits from the Brazilian trade that Portugal manages to make its war of the Restoration of Independence, after 60 years of an Iberian union with Spain (1580-1640). Thanks also to the Brazilian gold Lisbon has a new period of a quick prosperity, with King João V (1706-1750). The gold, that had arrived in tons, enabled the monarch to nect many magnificent works. Golden engraving, tiles, ceramics and other ornamental arts reach an exceptional quality in this period. To mitigate the thirst of Lisbon he built the *Aqueduct of Águas Livres*.

In 1755, a great calamity fell over the city: a violent earthquake destroyed the whole city centre and damaged seriously a number of buildings everywhere. However, this catastrophe would allow the Marquis of Pombal, the powerful minister of King José I (1750-1777), to rebuild the city according to modern urban conceptions. The city centre (*Baixa*) with wide, geometrical streets, flanked with simple and functional buildings. At the North End, a new *Rossio* and, by the Tagus, *Praça do Comércio*, with the ministries and, in the centre, King José's statue. The *Baixa Pombalina* became the real heart of the city, seat of the political and financial power.

*Lisbon Cathedral. The facade was restored some years ago, to give it back the strength and the simplicity of the original romance style (12th century).*

*Church of Santo António da Sé (18th century).*

13

Main portal of the Military Museum. In the distance, the Church Pantheon of Santa Engrácia.

Santa Engrácia: the waving of this wall expresses well the contradictory "movement" of the curve and countercurve, so characteristic of the baroque architecture.

At the end of the 18th century, Lisbon had the benefit of the vigorous action of the General Superintendent of the Police Pina Manique, who set up the first system of public illumination (with olive oil street lamps) and encouraged the building of the cathedral of opera in Portugal — The Theatre of São Carlos.

After the disturbance caused by Napoleon's invasions (1807-1811) and the fights related to the establishment of the liberal regime in Portugal (1820-1834), Lisbon went through a new period of expansion, in the second half of the 19th century.

The industrial areas of *Xabregas*, *Poço do Bispo* and *Alcântara*, where the factories were mixed with the workers' quarters, are urbanized.

In 1879, in the seat of the old Public Walk, the wide *Avenida da Liberdade* was built. The city started expanding to the North. New districts were built: *Estefânia*, *Campolide*, *Campo de Ourique*, where the bourgeoisie invested in buildings to let. In 1885, the building of King Eduardo VII Park started and, soon after, the urbanization of the so called "new avenues": Av. Fontes Pereira de Melo, A. da República, etc. A new city is born, turning its back on the Tagus. With about 300 thousand inhabitants in the end of the 19th century, Lisbon had more than 1 million nowadays (about 3 millions, taking into account the urban area of Greater Lisbon).

If we compare it with the great European or World metropolises, Lisbon is a small city, where life goes on quietly and the tourists meet nice and hospitable people, and a mild climate.

*...o views of the inside of ... Church of the Monas-... of Madre de Deus.*

*Church of the Conceição Velh
Manueline portal.*

*An old boat (frigate) of the T
gus.*

# LISBON

## Discovering the city

The visitor is invited to go for a walk that starts in the place where the city itself was born: St. George's Castle and the hillside of the primitive urban nucleus, going down from the Castle to the River Tagus.

The **Castle of Lisbon** sustained many alterations down the ages: it was a royal residence up to the 16th century. The earthquake of 1755 destroyed the old Palace of Alcaçova of St. George's Castle, of which a courtyard with a Gothic range of arches still remains. It is situated in the Ogival House, now a banqueting hall.

The visitor can admire, from the top of the towers and walls of St. George's Castle, one of the most superb panoramas over the city and the Tagus. Besides this, there are other excellent belvederes in Lisbon. Not far from St. George Castle, on an opposite hill, there is one of the most beautiful places in the whole city: the **Belvedere of Senhora do Monte**. From here your eyes reach the Castle, the Tagus, the bridge, *Cristo-Rei*; in front of you, the city centre and its continuation; to the North, the whole new city.

Another belvedere usually recommended for a visit is that of **Santa Luzia**, from which you can see most of the Tagus estuary and, at the bottom, one of the oldest and most picturesque districts in Lisbon — Alfama.

It is best to visit **Alfama** on foot. For centuries, the quarter has spread anarchically, with narrow streets, lanes, small staircases, picturesque houses and lively and noisy people.

The visitor may stroll along the narrow streets and lanes of Alfama: Rua da Adiça, Rua de S. Miguel, Rua da Judiaria (where, in the Middle Ages, one of the Jewish ghettoes in Lisbon was situated). Then the visitor can finally take a rest by going to one of the many characteristic restaurants of Alfama. There are many of them, scattered throughout the quarter, some popular, some luxurious.

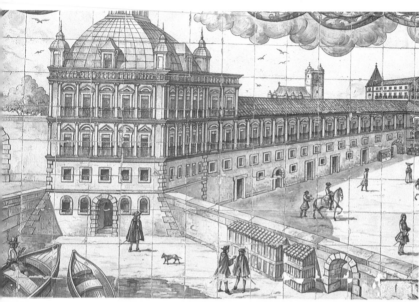

The Terreiro do Paço be
the earthquake of 1755.
18th century wall tile pa
in Santa Luzia's Church.

The Praça do Comércio
night.

*The* Praça do Comércio *as seen from the Tagus.*

*King José I's statue. In the distance, the Arch of Rua Augusta.*

*The Pillar Quay. On the left, a cacilheiro (ferry boat to Cacilhas, on the left bank of the river Tagus).*

*The City Hall building.*

◄

*One of the range of arches in* Praça do Comércio.

*An old tram. Lisbon is one of the few cities in the world that still use this nice and "clean" means of transport.*

*Lisbon is a city of slopes a*
*small staircases: a characteris*
*street in the popular quarter Bi*

*General view of the city cen*
*from the Largo da Biblioteca*

*The Lift of Santa Justa, built in the 19th century, is a magnificent example of the iron architecture. from the top you can enjoy an excellent scenery.*

*View of Rua Augusta.*

*Two views of Rossio.*

*Ruins of Convent of Car*
*(15th century). An archaeolo*
*cal museum is installed he*
*Concerts are usually held he*

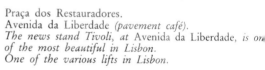

Praça dos Restauradores.
Avenida da Liberdade (*pavement café*).
*The news stand Tivoli*, at Avenida da Liberdade, *is one of the most beautiful in Lisbon.*
*One of the various lifts in Lisbon.*

Not far from Alfama, you can visit two magnificent monuments: the Church and Monastery of St. Vicente de Fora and the National Pantheon of Santa Engrácia.

The monumental complex of **St. Vicente de Fora** was built in the end of the 16th century, to replace another one that was older and more modest, also dedicated to the saint of Lisbon, St. Vicente. The name (*de Fora*) means outside the walls. It is a Mannerist building, of a period of transition between the Renaissance and the Baroque. It was built by Filipe II (King of Spain and Portugal). Filipe Terzi and Herrera, the architect of Escorial, worked together on the initial project. Inside the precious baroque altar, in the centre of the high altar stands out. The excellent tiles of the 18th century, either on the portal or in the cloisters, are also noteworthy. In the Monastery of St. Vicente you can also see the *Pantheon of the Braganças*, where the Portuguese monarchs of the last dynasty, who reigned between 1640 and 1910, are buried.

The **Church Pantheon of St. Engrácia** is a 17th century baroque building, of a central plan, whose construction has been interrupted for about 250 years. Only in 1966 the large dome, which is somewhat out of proportion, was finished.

Next to this magnificent building, on Tuesday and Saturday, the oldest and most popular market in Lisbon takes place — the **Flea Market** (*Feira da Ladra*). Here you may find the unexpected — an antique, a rare edition of a book, coins, old junk, furniture, clothes and shoes at prices that are usually much lower than in the shops.

The *Flea Market* is also one of the best places for the visitor to see the people of Lisbon — those who are selling and those who are buying. And feel the spontaneous joy, listen to people talking (although you cannot understand them), observe those people you do not usually meet in the monuments and museums.

Continuing on our way, we can now go down a little further: the **Monastery of Madre de Deus** is not far off. Although it has been enlarged and restored, the primitive nucleus dates from the early 16th century, and it was founded by Queen Leonor, King João II's wife. The church has a beautiful Manueline portico (restored), where King João II's symbol (the pelican) and Leonor's (the shrimping net) are detached. Inside the church is very rich: has some of the most beautiful golden engraving in the country and paintings and wall tiles equally precious. The *National Tile Museum* is set up in the rooms of the old Monastery nowadays.

*Church of S. Roque: the Chapel of St. John the Baptist. Richly decorated with Carrara marbles, tiles, golden carving, ivory and lapis lazuli (18th century).*

*A house with wall tiles (Largo da Trindade). The facades totally or partially covered with tiles are very popular in Lisbon.*

Now let us go westward, along the Tagus. Years ago, the Tagus was permanently crossed by characteristic boats, the *fragatas*, that carried all kinds of goods between the two river banks. They were very graceful boats, colourful painted, and with large triangular sails. Nowadays, the Tagus is more frequently crossed by big merchant ships and tankers that are going to be repaired at the Lisnave dockyards, situated on the left bank of the river Tagus.

Coming closer to *Praça do Comércio*, we should stop for a while near the **Casa dos Bicos**, an unusual 16th century building, with a facade made of stone hewn like a diamond end. It was the home of one of Afonso de Albuquerque's sons, governor of the Portuguese India. earthquake of 1755 destroyed the two upper levels. The restoration, accomplished in 1983, was the subject of some controversy, owing mainly to the new drawing of the windows.

Near the *Casa dos Bicos* is situated the **Churh of the Conceição Velha**, of the 16th century, whose excelent Manueline portal is all remains of the original building. Once again, the 18th century earthquake was responsible for the destruction of this temple, one of the finest in the city.

Not far away from the Church of the Conceição stands the **Cathedral** (*Sé de Lisboa*). It is the oldest church in Lisbon, whose building dates from the 12th century. The facafe (restored), the aisles and the transept are all that remains of the first Romance building. The high altar you can see nowadays is alread the third one. It was rebuilt in the 14th century, according to Gothic models and fell down in 1755, being replaced by the one you can see now, in the baroque style. The Gothic cloister was also damaged by the earthquake, but recently some restoring and stiffening works were undertaken. The *Sé* is closely connected with *Santo António*'s name, the saint of Lisbon. Santo António was born in the end of the 12th century right opposite the *Sé*, in the place where there is a church built to pay homage to the saint.

*...he National Theatre of São ...arlos at night.*

*...n 18th century fountain, at ...ua das Janelas Verdes. Many ...f these beautiful public ...untains were built all over ...e city, after the construc- ...on of the Aqueduct (Aque- ...to das Águas Livres).*

*...xcellent scenery over the ...ocks of Alcântara and the ...ver Tagus, from the gar- ...en opposite the National ...useum of Ancient Art.*

*The Tagus and the Bridge at sunset.*

*Two views of the Bridge.*

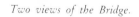

The Monument to Christ, the King (Monumento a Cristo-Rei) as seen from the Seminary of Almada.

Detail of the Monument to Christ, the King.

The Bridge as seen from the top of Ajuda.

QUEM NÃO

1º ALMIRANTE DA

A TRINETA QUE TRAZ

*Aerial view of Belém In the foreground, the Monument to br Discoveries. In the background, the Monastery of Jerónimos.*

*Cultural Center of Belém.*

*ur wall paintings by Al-*
*da Negreiros, at the*
*aritime Dock of*
*cântara (A.P.L.)*

*ew of the radiant foun-
n, near the Monastery of
rónimos, at night.*

► *e Monastery of Jerónimos.*

*atue of Afonso de Albu-
uerque. In the background,
e Palace of Belém, home
f the President of the Re-
blic.*

At last, we arrive at the square that is considered the most beautiful in Lisbon — the **Praça do Comércio**, situated on the site of the old *Terreiro do Paço*. It was located near the Palace (*Paço*) of the Ribeira, a royal residence until 1755: hence its name. On that date, the Palace of the Ribeira was completely destroyed. With the reconstruction undertaken by the Marquis of Pombal, this magnificent square, a real reception room of the city of Lisbon, was built. In the centre you can see the equestrian statue of the King José I, made by the great sculptor Machado de Castro. By the river, *Cais das Colunas* (the Pillar Quay), and on the other side, the great *Arch of the Augusta*, giving access to one of the three important streets of Pombal's city centre (the other two are *Rua do Ouro* and *Rua da Prata*). *Rua Augusta* is peopled nowadays by handicraft sellers, buskers, painters, etc. A *Baixa* (city centre) has some of the best shops in Lisbon. The headquarters of the most important Portuguese banks are also there.

The three streets of the *Baixa* and in the square that is the real heart of Lisbon: the **Rossio**. Even before the earthquake, the *Rossio* was already the *forum* of the city. In the middle is situated the statue of King Pedro IV, who, between 1832 and 1834, fought for the Liberal Revolution and made the parliamentary regime triumphant in Portugal. On the North side of square stands the National Theatre of D. Maria II, finished in 1846, according to the neoclassical models. Some pavement cafés allow the tourist to rest for a moment at Rossio while he is watching the constant coming and going of Lisboners, in one of the most crowded and cosmopolitan places in the city.

Let us visit now the **Praça dos Restauradores**, whose name is related to the restoration of the Portuguese independence, in 1640, after sixty years of Iberian union. The central obelisk reminds of the events of 1640. **Avenida da Liberdade**, one of the most beautiful streets in the city, with its gardens and pavement cafés, starts at the *Restauradores*.

The Church of the Monastery
of Jerónimos — inside.

Cloister of the Monastery of Jerónimos.

Two details of the decoration of
the cloister.

*The Tower of Belém.*

*Two details of the Tower Belém: sculpture of Our dy of Restelo and a sen box.*

*Monument to the Discoveries (general view and detail).*

*Gardens of the Palace of Ajuda.*

It is time for us now to visit another of the traditional quarters in Lisbon, the *Bairro Alto*. We can do it from *Restauradores*, by using one of the most characteristic means of transport in the city: the *cable car*. There are several of these lifts, yellow like the trams. The lift of the *Glória* will take us to the **Belvedere of St. Pedro de Alcântara**, from where you can admire another magnificent panorama over Lisbon, now on the opposite side to that we already know. The rows of houses, seen at the sunset, is one of the most fascinating sights in all the city.

Right at its side is **Bairro Alto**, with its narrow streets and various restaurants and *casas de fado* (restaurants where the national song *fado* is sung). The *fado* is a fatalistic song, usually sad, sentimental, that tells about destiny, unhappy love affairs and yearning. It is the traditional song of Lisbon whose origins seem to be in the colonial Brazil. It is usually accompanied by the Portuguese guitar and the *viola* and must be listened to in absolute silence. Besides *Bairro Alto*, the *fado* can be enjoyed in other houses at *Alfama* or *Madragoa*, other picturesque quarters in the city.

Before going down again towards the river, you should visit **the Church of St. Roque**, a Jesuit building of the end of 16th century. Decorated with paintings, wall tiles and golden engravings, it is one of the best examples of the Mannerism and of the Baroque in Lisbon. Specially noteworthy is the *Chapel of St. John the Baptist*, a very rich gift from King João V, built with the gold coming from Brazil and that cost a fortune.

Close by you can see the **Convent of Carmo**, a Gothic building of the beginning of the 15th century. Ruined by the earthquake of 1755, it has never been rebuilt. Its elegant ogival arches, supporting a vault formed by the open sky, are a natural element of the landscape of Lisbon nowadays.

Following the tour suggested to the visitor, it is now essential to walk along the **Chiado**, another one the most active commercial areas in Lisbon. Two magnificent playhouses — *Teatro Municipal de S. Luís* and *Teatro Nacional de S. Carlos* are situated here as well. The latter was built in the end of the 18th century and outside is a simple, well-balanced and neoclassical building. Inside, it has a very rich decoration in golden engraving and painted plaster. With an excellent acoustics it is usually used for opera performances, music and ballet.

Getting back to the Tagus, we come closer to *Ponte 25 de Abril* (25th April Bridge). This impressive engineering was concluded in 1966 and makes the connection North-South, joining Lisbon to the busy region of Setúbal. Crossing it the visitor can make his way to the excellent beaches of *Costa da Caparica* or visit the **Statue to Christ, the King** (*Monumento a Cristo-Rei*), in Almada. From the bridge or, even better, from the top of *Cristo-Rei*, you will enjoy the most dazzling sight over the city of Lisbon.

Near the bridge we advise the visitor to enter, for a moment, the *Maritime Docks* of *Alcântara* and *Rocha Conde de Óbidos*. Here you can admire the magnificent frescoes painted by *Almada Negreiros*, one of the most representative Portuguese modern painters.

Basilica of Estrela: the dome, as
seen from the garden.

Detail on the terrace of the Basilica (flamboyant stone orna-
ments).

◄

Basilica of Estrela: general view
and bell tower.

Two of the most extraordinary examples of the Portuguese art of all times are situated at **Belém** — the Monastery of Jerónimos and the Tower of Belém are now considered part of the cultural heritage of all mankind as they have been declared world monuments and placed under the protection of UNESCO.

The **Monastery of Jerónimos** was built by King Manuel I, protector and patron of the arts, in a period when Portugal started taking advantage of the trade of the Eastern spices, after Vasco da Gama had discovered the sea passage to India (1498). The Monastery of Jerónimos has two splendid richly decorated portals. Entering the church, you feel a dazzling and wonderful sensation, for its vastness, structural originality and exuberant decoration. The three naves being all of the same height, coverd by a single vault, form a hall-church. Thin octagonal pillars, decorated in the Renaissance and Plateresque styles, support the multi veined vaulting and have the appearance of palm trees. The *cloister* of the Monastery of Jerónimos is not only the most valuable jewel of the monument but, in the eyes of many historians, is also considered one of the most beautiful cloisters in the world. For the balance and harmony of its proportions, the originality of its structure, its abundant and inventive decoration it stands unique.

The **Tower of Belém** is the most symbolic Portuguese monument of the times of the sea discoveries. It was built by King Manuel I to protect the bar of the river Tagus. The Tower did not take long to be finished: it started in 1515 and was completed in 1521. The works were directed by the architect *Francisco de Arruda*.

The tower is formed principally of two distinct parts: the *stronghold* and the *donjon* or *keep*. On the terrace of the stronghold you can admire a sculpture of Our Lady of Belém. In the corners there are six graceful sentry-boxes covered with sectioned domes. From this terrace there is an excellent view over the southern side of the Tower, with its marvellous long balcony. Above, an enormous royal coat of arms and two armillary spheres, King Manuel I's symbols.

Near the Tower of Belém you can see the **Monument to the Discoveries**. Here

arquês de Pombal Square.
the foreground, an exam-
of the beautiful and tra-
ional sidewalks in Lisbon,
th black and white dra-
ngs, made with rocks
nds in the area (limestone
d schist).

tail of the statue of the
arquis of Pombal.

e Parliament (palace of
Bento).

nd in Campo Grande Gar-
ns.

queduto das Águas Livres
queduct of the Free Waters).
th century.

ne of the most modern urban
mplexes in Lisbon — Amorei-
s.

can be found representations of many of those Portuguese who, according to the poet Luís de Camões, *gave new worlds to the World*. On the pavement, near the staircase to the Monument, a gigantic marble mariner's compass can be admired. It has got a planisphere in the middle, where the most important regions disco-vered by the Portuguese in the 15th and 16th centuries are marked. An elevator takes the visitors to the terrace, from where you can gaze over the whole area of Belém and its superb monuments.

At *Estrela* you can admire one of the most beautiful buildings ever built in Portugal in the 18th century — the **Basilica of Estre-la,** of predominant neoclassical lines. It has an excellent dome, from where you can gaze at most of the city.

From Estrela, crossing the garden with the same name, you will reach **Marquês de Pombal Square** quickly. The statue, in the middle of this circular Plaza, was erected already in the early 20th century, paying homage to King José's powerful minister. The statue faces *Avenida da Liberdade*. Behind it you can see *Eduardo VII Park*. The **Cool Greenhouse** (*Estufa Fria*), a green and fresh tropical garden, full of beautiful and rare species, is integrated in this park.

Finaly the visitor can now walk along the wide avenues of the most recent quarters of Lisbon. *Avenida da República* leads you to **Campo Grande**, with its gardens, ponds, tennis courts, pavement cafés and restaurants. The *Classical University* and the *National Library* are situated nearby. Not far away you can see the stadiums of the biggest clubs in Lisbon — *Benfica* and *Sporting*.

The **Bull Ring of Campo Pequeno** is also situated near Avenida da República. Bullfighting, one of the most traditional shows in the Peninsula, takes place here. To the contrary of what happens in Spain the bulls are not killed during the show in Portugal. On the other hand, Potuguese bullfights do not include matadors, but only horsemen and *forcados*. The horseman shows his art thanks to well trained horses, deceiving the bull and thrusting *banderillas* in its back without being touched. In the end of the bullfighting the *forcados* take the bull by the horns, facing it bravely in the middle of the bull ring.

At the end of this journey, many things are still to be seen. The visitor noticed, probably, places and people that were not referred to here. Lisbon is a rich and varied city and it is difficult to "capture" it in a few pages. With time and imagination you will discover another city: that of the windows and verandas of forged iron; of the wall tiled houses; that of the chestnut and ice cream sellers; the bright and tranquil Lisbon of Saturday or Sunday mornings. With a bit of luck the foreign visitor may even find inLisbon things that have disappeared completely in other European cities: a cart being pulled by a sluggish donkey, or even a flock of sheep crossing a suburban avenue. And you may discover small restaurants and popular wine bars, where you can eat sardines and drink a glass of wine. And meet friendly and hospitable people who are always kind to visitors. Lisbon is an old city, but it always looks new.

*...rtuguese bullfight: the ...orseman, dressed as an ...8th century's nobleman, ...ghts the bull always on ...rseback. After defying the ...ll, he moves in front of it, ...rusts a fluke in and tries ... escape without being tou-...ed.*

*...ne of the most exciting ...oments of the Portuguese ...llfight: taking the bull by ...e horns (pega). The forca-...os take the bull by the ...nd with courage and va-...r. They are usually ama-...urs and take the bulls only ...r pleasure.*

*...ull ring at Campo Pequeno.*

# LISBON

## City of Museums

Portugal is a country with more than eight centuries of history. The memory of its antiquity can be found in monuments, some of which the visitor of Lisbon already knows. But the museums also keep small parts of that collective memory, without which the peoples do not recognise themselves as a whole. And Lisbon is a city with many museums.

The *National Museum of Ancient Art* is installed in an old 12th century palace. It is the first museum in the country for the quantity and quality of its heritage: painting, sculpture and pieces of ornamental art. Besides an excelent collection of Portuguese art, it has also some exceptional foreign works of art, among which Bosch's triptych *The Temptations of St. Anton* and Albrecht Dürer's *St. Jerome* stand out. As regards national painting, *St. Vicente de Fora Panels*, a 15th century poliptych, ascribed to Nuno Gonçalves, is outstanding.

The National Museum of Ancient Art has also some remarkable pieces of sculpture, tapestry, furniture, ceramics, illumination and jewelry.

The *Calouste Gulbenkian Museum* keeps the valuable collection that belonged to the maker of the Foundation that has his name. Being part of a magnificent park, the Gulbenkian Museum has objects of art that come from ancient Egypt and go to the great impressionist painters of the 19th century. The departments of Islamic art, eastern ceramics, 17th and 18th century furniture and painting of several schools and periods.

*Panel of the Prince. I[s] one of the six that make [the] Pannels of St. Vicente [de] Fora (National Museum [of] Ancient Art), a masterp[iece] of Portuguese painting of 15th century. In this pa[nel] you can see Prince Her[i]que, the beginner of mar[iti]me discoveries in the 1[5th] century (on the right, with [a] large hat).*

*17th century tile panel. [Na]tional Tile Museum.*

*The Monstrance of Bel[ém] (National Museum of A[n]cient Art). King Manue[l] had this exceptional 1[6th] century piece of Goth[ic] -Manueline jewellery m[ade] with the first gold brou[ght] from the Far East by Va[sco] da Gama.*

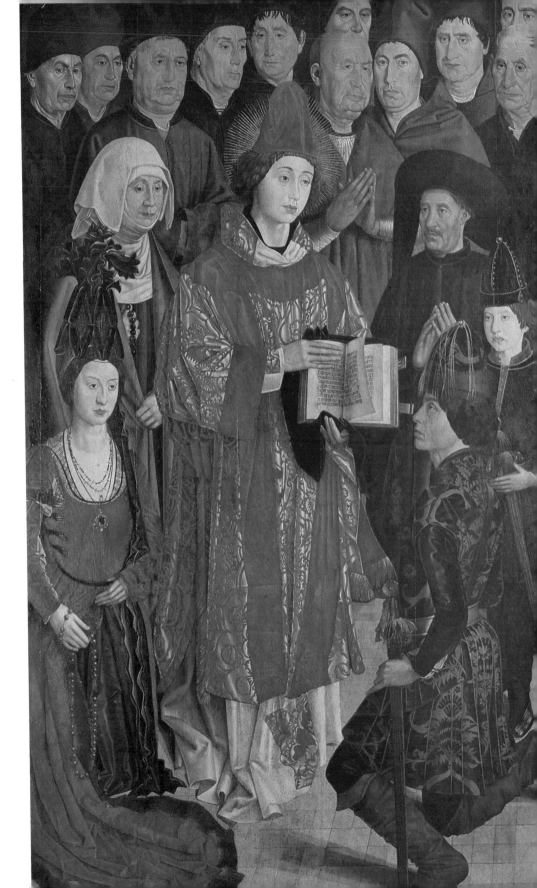

*View of the Museum of Coaches.*

The *National Museum of the Coaches*, at Belém, has the largest variety and complete collection of the kind all over the world.

Installed in rooms of the Monastery of Jerónimos the *Archaeological Museum* has a vast collection of pieces that confirm not only the pre and protohistorical times, but also the period of the Roman occupation of the Peninsula. It also keeps one of the collections of pre-Roman jewelry in the world.

The *Museum of Ethnology* has excelent collections of Brazilian and African art and possesses, in its depots, a real treasure of objects related to the traditions and the popular culture of Portugal.

Portugal is a country of sailors and fishermen. Its history is intimately connected with life at sea. The *Navy Museum* possesses an exceptional number of pieces showing all that activity.

The *Military Museum*, at Santa Apolónia, is installed in the old arsenal of the Army, in a 18th century building. The two large portals are specially noteworthy. Inside, a varied and rich collection of guns and instruments related to military activities.

The Portuguese inherited the taste and the Arabian tradition for the wall tile. The cool of the tiles was suitable for the Portuguese climate. For that reason there is an exceptional variety and quality of wall tiles in Portugal. Many of them are still on the where they were placed. Others have been preserved in the *Tile Museum*, in the rooms of the old Monastery of Madre de Deus.

The *Museum of Contemporany Art* possesses works of art (specially painting) after 1850. Some of the greatest Portuguese modern painters, such as Silva Porto, Malhoa, Columbano, Almada Negreiros, etc., are represented here.

Situated at Campo Grande, in the old Pimenta Palace, the *Museum of the City* tries to preserve the memory of Lisbon. It is essential to visit it, if you want to know Lisbon and its history well.

The *National Costume Museum* and the *Museum of the Theatre*, situated in the pleasant park of the *Monteiro-Mor*, in the area of *Paço do Lumiar*, are two of the most recent museums in Lisbon. Excellently organized, they have a large number of objects on display.

*An 18th century's dress. National Museum of the Dress.*

*O Fado. Painting by José Malhoa (19th century) in the Museum of the City. It shows a fado singer accompanied with a Portuguese guitar.*

Estoril: a view of Tamariz bea

The Calouste Gulbenkian Museum. Above: panel of Islamic tiles and jewel by R. Lalique. On the right: The Boy and the Cherries, by Manet.

# LISBON

## The Suburbs

The visitor to Lisbon has at his disposal, in an area of about thirty kilometres, an exceptional variety of marvellous places to see — excellent beaches, fresh timbered hills, magnificent palaces, the cut out and steep Atlantic coast. There are plenty of good hotels, characteristic restaurants, golf courses and tennis courts as well.

On the bank of the Tagus, all along *Costa da Caparica*, there are many kilometres of beaches of fine clean sand, beaten by waters that are not polluted. If you want to go a little farther to the south, *Sesimbra*, *Arrábida* and *Tróia* are real paradisical oases.

Going along the river Tagus, on its right bank, you will not take long to reach **Estoril**, one of the principal resorts in the country. At Estoril, besides excellent hotels and restaurants there is the beach, the casino, the autodrome, the peaceful and green avenues, the sophisticated villas and houses of one of the most important areas in the suburbs of the capital.

Close by is **Cascais**, a little town of fishermen, famous for its mild bay and its magnificent restaurants. It is worth while visiting the *Museum of the Counts Castro Guimarães*, that keeps, among many valuable pieces, the manuscript where the picture of Lisbon in the 16th century included in this book (page 4), can be found.

Going on along the coast, we arrive at **Boca do Inferno**, a curious and impressive grotto dug out of the rocks by the gigantic strength of the wind and the sea.

Soon after that you will see the **Beach of Guincho**, wild and windy, having exceptional conditions for the practice of windsurfing.

The *hills of Sintra* are the majestic background of this beach. As we climb the road that winds round the hill, the horizons enlarge and Guincho, Cascais, Estoril, Lisbon and, in the distance, the mountain of Arrábida come into right. The view is dazzling. Soon after you get to the steep and wild end of *Cape of Roca*, the most westerly in Europe.

**Sintra** is one of the most beautiful sites in the world. It is exceptionally situated, near Lisbon and the sea, on the slope of a cool and densely forested hill, where Nature has exceeded itself to create a *"glorious Eden"*, to use Byron's words.

For many centuries, and thanks to its climate, shady woods and natural parks stocked with beautiful and unique varieties have grown in Sintra. Its suburbs are just like the jewels that ornament a royal crown: the excellent beaches of *Praia Grande* and *Praia das Maças*; *Azenhas de Mar*, an amazing white and sunny crib; the fertile valley of *Colares*, with its farms, its famous wines, its luxuriant green. In Sintra you cannot miss climbing up to *Cruz Alta*, 540 metres high; going to *Peninha*, one of the most beautiful and rocky places in the mountain; to *Convento dos Capuchos*, a humble monastery built in the middle of rocks and century old trees; going to the mild and bucolic *Lagoa Azul* (Blue Pond); visiting the *Palaces of Seteais* and of *Monserrate*. The *Castle of the Moors* is one of the most important monuments in Sintra. Deeply rooted in the massive granite it seems to be born from the earth. From the battlements you can look at one of the most beautiful and majestic sceneries in the whole area.

Finally, in Sintra, you should visit the *National Palace* and the *Palace of the Pena*. The Palace of Sintra, situated in the ancient site of the little town, is one of the most remarkable civil building in Portugal, whose construction started in the Arabian period. However, the most important parts date from the 15th and 16th century. It has exceptionally beautiful rooms, decorated with one of the best collection of walltiles in Portugal. Some of the ceilings and the furniture in the Palace are equally remarkable.

*...ra: Palace of Monser-... . It is a Palace of an ...bian architectural in-...nce in the middle of a ...gnificent natural park ...owed with some unique ...*

*...ra: Palace of Seteais. ... old 18th century ma-...house, that belonged ...he Marquis of Marial-... is a luxurious hotel ...adays.*

*...cais: view of the bay ... of a beach.*

On the top of the hill, in a densely forested site, it is situated a Palace and Castle like those of the fairy tales, the *Palace of the Pena*. It dates from the 19th century and it was built by the Prince Consort Fernando II, Queen Maria II's husband, in the ruins of a 16th century small Manueline monastery.

Prince Fernando commited Baron Eschewege, a fellow countryman of his, to build a romantic building. He joined there Gothic, Manueline, Moorish and German influences.

On the way back to Lisbon, you can still visit the *Palace of Queluz*. It is a building of the end of the 18th century, in the transition from the baroque to the neoclassicism. Many people call it "the small Portuguese Versailles".

The journey around Lisbon and its suburbs has come to end. But Portugal is musch more than Lisbon. We hope that you have enjoyed this visit and we are sure that you will be very much interested in visiting the other parts of the country (if you do not know them yet).

*Sintra: Palace of the Pena. At a distance, this romantic palace and castle seems to be the natural continuation of the mountain where it stands and of the involving vegetation.*

*National Palace of Sintra.*

*National Palace of Queluz.*